# *Celebrate*
# Hindu Festivals

Series editor: Jan Thompson

Dilip Kadodwala
Paul Gateshill

Heinemann
LIBRARY

294.5
Kadodwala

Designed by Sue Clarke
Illustrated by Jeff Edwards and Lesley Harler
Color reproduction by Track QSP
Printed in Hong Kong by
Wing King Tong Company Limited.

02 01
10 9 8 7 6 5 4 3

**Library of Congress Cataloging-in-Publication
Data**
Kadodwala, Dilip.
  Hindu festivals / Dilip Kadodwala, Paul Gateshill.
    p.    cm. -- (Celebrate)
  Includes index.
  ISBN 0-431-06966-2 (lib. bdg.)
  1. Fasts and feasts--Hinduism--Juvenile literature.
2. Hinduism--Customs and practices--Juvenile
literature.    I. Gateshill, Paul, 1954-    .    II.
Title.    III. Series: Celebrate (Crystal Lake, Ill.)
BL1239.72.K33    1997
294.5'36--dc21                                97-2412
                                                    CIP

**Acknowledgments**
The Publishers would like to thank the following for
permission to reproduce photographs.

Anit Lakhani's Studio, Leicester: p. 4; International
Association of the Vrindaban Research Institute, School of
Oriental and African Studies, University of London: p. 7; E.
Nesbitt: p. 8; David Rose: p. 10; Trip/F Good: p. 11; David
Rose: p.12; Ann & Bury Peerless: p. 13; Ann & Bury Peerless:
p.14; David Rose: p. 15; Circa Photo Library/John Smith: p.
16; Ann & Bury Peerless: p.17; Trip/Dinodia: p.18;
Trip/Dinodia: p. 20; Ann & Bury Peerless: p. 21; Trip/Dinodia:
p. 22; Trip/H Rogers: p. 24; David Rose: p. 25; David Rose: p.
26; David Rose: p. 27; Ann & Bury Peerless: p. 28; Phil & Val
Emmett: p. 30; Trip/H Rogers: p. 31; Phil & Val Emmett: p. 32;
p. 33 by courtesy of the Board of Trustees of the Victoria &
Albert Museum; Ann & Bury Peerless: p. 34; Trip/Dinodia: p.
35; Trip/Dinodia: p. 36; David Rose: p. 37; Panos Pictures/
Jean-Leo Dugast: p. 38; David Rose: p. 40; Trip/H Rogers: p.
42; Trip/Dinodia: p. 43.

Cover photograph reproduced with permission of Eye
Ubiquitous/David Cummings.

Our thanks to Denise Cush and Helen Chandra for their
comments in the preparation of this book.

**The authors would like to thank their families,
in particular Devan, Mark, Viren, and Susannah,
to whom this book is dedicated.**

# Contents

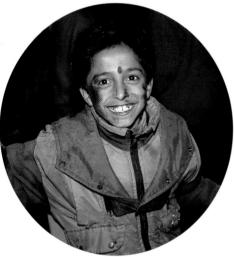

# Introduction

This is Devan. He is seven years old. He goes to an elementary school in Chicago.

" In my school there are boys and girls who belong to many different religions. I think this is good. It gives us a chance to celebrate many festivals! My favorite festival is called Divali. I like to take special candies to school and share them with everybody. "
– *Devan*

Divali is just one of many Hindu festivals. This book shows you how some of the main ones are celebrated and why they are important to Hindus all over the world.

## A religion with many branches

One way you can understand Hinduism is to think about a big tree with many roots and branches. Some branches are short and others long, yet it is still growing! This picture of a tree is a way of saying that Hinduism has many beliefs about God, the world, and the humans in it.

*Brahman* is a Hindu word for God. Hindus believe that Brahman is everywhere and in everything. Although Hindus believe that there is one God, Brahman can be pictured in many different forms, as many different gods and goddesses. So there are many stories of gods and goddesses. Many Hindu festivals are about these gods and goddesses.

## Hinduism in history

Hinduism is one of the world's oldest religions. People who follow this religion are called *Hindus*. Hindu beliefs about God and how human beings should live have grown over a long period of time. So there was not one person who began this religion. It also does not have just one "special" holy book. Hindus call their religion **"sanatan dharma."** This means "eternal religion." The word *eternal* means "without ever ending."

The roots of Hinduism began in India. Most Hindus live in India. Others live here in the United States and in Africa, the United Kingdom, Canada, and Asia.

*Om, sometimes spelled* aum, *is the sacred sound or word for God. Hindus say it at the start of their prayers.*

*There are three main appearances of Brahman: Brahma, who made the world; Vishnu, who protects the world; and Shiva, who destroys it, so that it can be made again.*

# Festivals

Hindus have many festivals through the year. They sometimes say that it feels as if every day is a festival day!

A diagram of a Hindu calendar and the main festivals

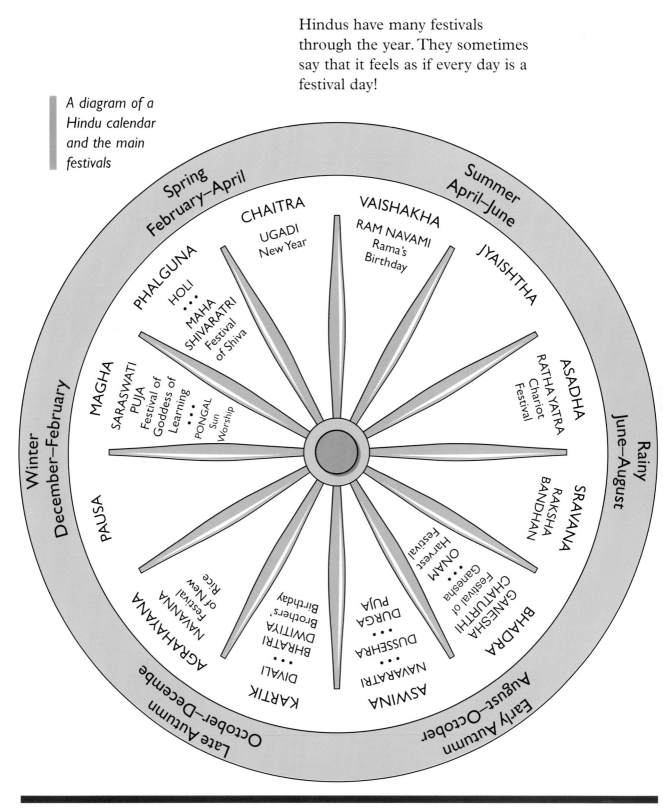

Spring
February–April

Summer
April–June

Rainy
June–August

Early Autumn
August–October

Late Autumn
October–December

Winter
December–February

CHAITRA
UGADI
New Year

VAISHAKHA
RAM NAVAMI
Rama's
Birthday

JYAISHTHA

PHALGUNA
HOLI
• • •
MAHA
SHIVARATRI
Festival
of Shiva

ASADHA
RATHA YATRA
Chariot
Festival

MAGHA
SARASWATI
PUJA
Festival of
Goddess of
Learning
• • •
PONGAL
Sun
Worship

SRAVANA
RAKSHA
BANDHAN

PAUSA

BHADRA
GANESHA
CHATURTHI
Festival of
Ganesha
• • •
ONAM
Harvest
Festival

AGRAHAYANA
NAVANNA
Festival
of New
Rice

KARTIK
DIVALI
• • •
BHRATRI
DWITIYA
Brothers'
Birthday

ASWINA
NAVARATRI
• • •
DUSSEHRA
• • •
DURGA
PUJA

*A page from a Hindu holy book, showing text written in Sanskrit*

## The Hindu year

Hindu calendars are based on the movement of the moon. A Hindu calendar has 12 lunar months. Each month is divided into a "bright half" (from the new moon to the full moon) and a "dark half" (from the full moon to the next new moon). As Hindus use a lunar calendar, the dates of festivals change from year to year. The Western calendar is based on the movement of the sun. It has 365 days. The Hindu calendar has about 354 days.

In parts of India some festivals are celebrated at the same time, but in different ways. It is even more confusing when the same festival is called by a different name! For instance, the festival of *Dassehra* in northern India is *Durgapuja* in eastern India.

The diagram shows when the main Hindu festivals occur in the lunar year. The **Sanskrit** names of the months are given, as well as the names of the months used in the West. Sanskrit is the name of a very old Indian language. For Hindus, Sanskrit is a sacred language. Holy books are written in this language. Prayers are also said in Sanskrit.

# Preparations for Divali

Divali celebrations in a mandir (temple). Light plays an important part in Hindu worship.

“I really look forward to Divali each year. My brothers and sisters and I get really excited. We give each other presents and send cards to our relatives all over the world. My favorite part is when we fill the house with *diva* lamps. We turn all the lights out and light all the divas and it looks great.”
*– Alka*

Alka lives with her big family in India. Like all Hindu children she looks forward to Divali.

## What is Divali?

Divali is one of the best known Hindu festivals. It is a New Year festival and takes place in the fall, around October or November. Like many Hindu festivals, Divali has many parts. It is celebrated in various ways in different countries of the world. As a New Year festival, Divali is about new beginnings.

Hindu families clean their homes from top to bottom. The houses are then decorated with glitter and tinsel. Little clay lamps called **divas** are lit and placed in the windows and outside the front door. This is to attract the attention of Lakshmi and to welcome her to the house. Lakshmi is the goddess of wealth and all Hindus hope that she will visit their homes and bless them with a prosperous new year. Divali is also a time for people to pay off all their debts and sort out everything to do with money and business. At Divali, greetings cards are sent to friends and relatives.

## Lakshmi and the lotus flower

If you look carefully at the image of Lakshmi you can see that she is sitting atop a lotus flower. She is also holding lotus flowers in her hands. These flowers are very popular in Hindu art. They represent purity. Lotus flowers are similar to water lilies. You may have noticed that they look so fresh and beautiful. They are so clean, even though they grow out of the muddy water.

Lakshmi's other hands are in a gesture of giving. She is the goddess of wealth, and here she is sharing her wealth with everybody who worships her. Lakshmi is kind and generous. Many Hindus worship her as a mother goddess.

*An image of the goddess Lakshmi*

# Divali Decorations

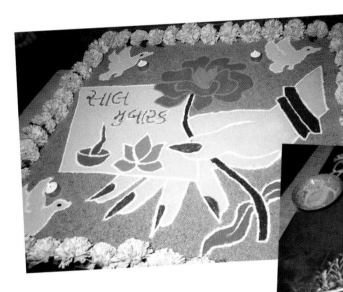

It takes a lot of skill to make rangoli patterns like these.

" At Divali, we make these lovely rangoli patterns. We use rangoli patterns in our homes and in the *mandir*. The mandir is a special name for our place of worship. Some people are really clever and make fantastic rangoli patterns of scenes from the Ramayana, like the picture on the right. "
– *Alka*

During the festival of Divali, Alka loves to make **rangoli** patterns. Her mother and aunts also get very excited about making patterns.

## Rangoli and mendhi patterns

Rangoli patterns are used to decorate homes and mandirs at important festival times. They are a special way of welcoming visitors. A pattern may be geometric, or in the form of a fruit, flower, tree, or religious Hindu figures. If the rangoli patterns are really beautiful, then perhaps even Lakshmi will visit! Hindus believe that when Lakshmi visits, she leaves her wealth wherever she goes.

*Rangoli patterns being made on a street in India*

Rangoli patterns can be made with colored rice or with different colored sands or chalks. You may want to try to make your own rangoli pattern.

At Divali, Hindus may also decorate their hands and feet with **mendhi** patterns, to make themselves look beautiful. These patterns are painted with a brown dye called *henna*, which lasts for several days. Mendhi patterns are also used at Hindu and Muslim weddings.

## Sharing candies

During the festival of Divali the sharing of food is especially important. When people visit family and friends they take a tray of candies with them. Sometimes, when Hindus return home, they have more of these candies on the tray than they had at the start of their visits! One of the candies eaten is called *barfi*, which is like fudge. You will find a recipe for barfi on page 15.

### Making rangoli patterns

*First of all, you will need to find a piece of cardboard or a wooden board. Make your design on the board with pencil or charcoal. Rather than colored rice, it may be better to use colored chalk or glitter. You will need to be very careful when you sprinkle the different colors onto the board. If you want to be able to carry it around, you will need to put some glue onto the board before you sprinkle on the colors.*

# Prince Rama and Sita

> **In our school we are studying Divali. We are preparing a dance to tell the story of Ramayana. This is when the Lord Rama defeats Ravana, the ten-headed demon. I am going to be Hanuman, the monkey king.**
> *– Alka*

*Children dancing a scene from the Ramayana*

One of the major features of Divali is the story of Prince Rama and his wife Sita. This famous story comes from a book called the **Ramayana**, and is popular among Hindus everywhere. An important part of Divali is when this story is told through dance or drama. Here is a brief outline of the story.

## Rama's story

When Prince Rama and his wife Sita were sent away from their country, they spent many years living in the forest with Lakshmana, who was Rama's brother. Ravana, the ten-headed demon, kidnapped Sita and kept her a prisoner on his island, Lanka. Rama called upon his friend Hanuman, the monkey king. With the help of all the animals of the forest, Hanuman built a bridge from India to the island of Lanka so that Rama and Lakshmana could cross.

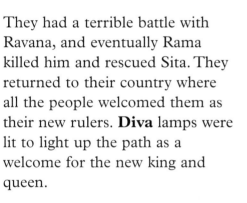
*Here is a picture of Rama and Sita, together with Lakshmana and Hanuman*

They had a terrible battle with Ravana, and eventually Rama killed him and rescued Sita. They returned to their country where all the people welcomed them as their new rulers. **Diva** lamps were lit to light up the path as a welcome for the new king and queen.

This story shows how good will always conquer evil. Hindus believe that the diva light will always chase away the darkness.

## Why Rama is important

In the picture, Prince Rama is seated on a throne in the middle. He is usually shown with a bow in his hand. Hanuman is often shown kneeling in front of Rama. This is because Rama is not just a prince. Hindus believe that Rama is the God Vishnu, who has come to the earth to save the world from the wicked demon Ravana. You can read more about Vishnu's appearances on earth on page 33.

# The Meaning of Holi

> **This is an image of Lord Krishna. Here he is with Radha, his favorite *gopi* (milkmaid). He is holding a flute, because he used to play beautiful music to make the *gopis* dance. I always feel happy when I think of Krishna.**
> – *Meena*

*An image of Krishna with Radha*

Meena is nine years old. She lives with her family in Bombay, India. They believe in Lord Krishna, who is worshiped in a special way during the festival of Holi.

## What is Holi?

Holi is a popular and joy-filled Hindu festival. It takes place in the winter or early spring, during February or March. There are two different stories which are remembered at Holi. One is about Krishna and the other is about Prahlad.

During Holi Hindus go to the **mandir** and worship Krishna. There may even be dances telling the story of Krishna or Prahlad. This worship is known as **puja** by Hindus. A puja tray is used to show devotion to the images of the gods.

*A puja tray
with offerings*

There is a bell which is rung to show that worship has begun. There is incense to make an offering of pleasant sweet smells. Food is offered to the god and to the people. A lamp called an **arti** lamp is lit. In this way all the senses are involved: sound, smell, taste, touch, and sight.

After worship in the mandir, everybody goes outside to light a huge bonfire. Special foods are eaten, especially coconuts.

## Worshiping the elements

Natural elements such as water and fire are important to Hindus. Fire is worshiped as God or is seen as God's power. During worship, Hindus light a **diva**, which is a kind of lamp. A diva is made with a wick. A wick is made from twisted cotton wool. It is dipped in **ghee**. Ghee is melted butter. The wick is placed in a small clay or brass pot and is then lit.

During arti, which is a special prayer sung by worshipers, five cotton wicks are lit. These five flames stand for our five senses.

### A recipe for coconut barfi

*Here is a recipe for a candy called coconut barfi, which is often made at Holi. Remember to ask an adult to help you make this candy.*

**Ingredients:**
*$6\frac{1}{4}$ oz. evaporated milk*
*$5\frac{1}{4}$ oz. dried coconut*
*$3\frac{1}{2}$ oz. granulated sugar*

**Equipment:**
*Saucepan and wooden spoon*

**Instructions:**
*Pour the milk into the saucepan. Add the sugar and heat on a low flame. Stir occasionally. Bring to a boil and simmer until the milk has reduced by half. Stir in half the coconut and continue stirring for 5 minutes, then add the rest of the coconut. Remove ingredients from the pan and spread on a greased cookie sheet. Leave to cool and then cut into squares.*

# Lord Krishna

Deepak, aged 11, lives in New York. This is what he says about Holi.

"Holi is one of my favorite times of the year. It's the only time I can get really dirty and not be scolded by my parents. My brothers, sisters, and cousins all come to my house. We change into our oldest clothes and go into the backyard. This is where the fun starts! We squirt bottles full of colored water and we have a huge water fight. You should see us! After a few minutes we are all covered in different colors. Even our hair ends up green, yellow, red, and blue. My mom and dad are too scared to come outside, so they watch us from the house. Last year my uncle came out with a box of colored powder and attacked all of us. He was covered from head to toe when we had finished spraying him!

We play this game to remember when Lord Krishna was young. He was always playing tricks on everybody, especially Radha and her friends, the *gopis* (milkmaids). Krishna is God and this game reminds us that God likes to laugh and have fun, too!"

– *Deepak*

*This is Deepak enjoying the fun of Holi.*

## Krishna's story

The tradition of tricks and games at Holi reminds Hindus of stories about Lord Krishna. There is one particular story which is remembered.

It was a lovely spring day and Krishna was walking by the river with his favorite companion, Radha, and with her friends, the **gopis**. They were milkmaids and Krishna would often meet with them and make them dance to his flute. On this occasion Krishna decided to have some real fun and threw some colored dye over Radha. She threw some over Krishna and soon everybody was covered from head to foot in colored dye.

This might seem a weird story to remember each year in a festival. It has a deeper meaning for Hindus, however. It reminds them that Krishna, who is God, wants a special, close relationship with all those who worship him.

*A painting of Krishna and Radha, with the gopis watching. Krishna is playing the flute.*

# Prahlad

## Bonfire celebrations

Rakesh, aged eight, thinks that Holi is his favorite festival. This is what he says about it.

" I love the bonfire at Holi. After *arti* in the mandir we all go outside and enjoy the bonfire celebrations. We've been collecting wood for a long time before Holi, so it's always huge. After the ceremony, our brahmin lights the fire and holy water is poured onto the wood. People throw all sorts of things into the fire. They throw candies, dates, popcorn, rice, and even money. We also place coconuts on the edge of the fire and eat them later. They're delicious! The bonfire reminds us of when the king's wicked sister Holika tried to burn Prahlad on a bonfire but God saved him from the flames. After the bonfire party we go home and have another feast with our family. "

– *Rakesh*

*Hindus in India enjoying a Holi bonfire*

## Prahlad's story

A bonfire is made at Holi to remind Hindus that good always wins over evil. The following story is told:

There was once a king who did not believe in God. In fact, he wanted everybody to worship him in God's place. He had a son called Prahlad who refused to worship his father, because he knew that the king was not God.

The king was furious and ordered Prahlad to be thrown into a pit filled with poisonous snakes. Everybody thought that Prahlad would be killed, but Lord Vishnu protected him and he came out of the pit unharmed. The king was even more determined to kill him and arranged for Prahlad to be trampled to death by wild elephants while he was sleeping. Again Vishnu came to his rescue and he escaped unharmed.

Then the king's wicked sister, who was called Holika, took Prahlad onto the top of a huge bonfire. She had magic powers and could not be harmed by the flames. She thought that Prahlad would be burned alive, but again the God Vishnu protected him. Holika's magic powers were destroyed and she disappeared in the flames.

*Holika leads Prahlad into the flames. Prahlad is saved.*

# Raksha Bandhan

*Raksha Bandhan* is a festival for brothers and sisters. It takes place on the full moon day of Shravana (July–August). *Raksha* means "protection" and *Bandhan* means "to tie." It is a festival celebrated by adults, as well as children. A special ceremony takes place in which the sister ties a **rakhi** on her brother's wrist. A rakhi is a kind of woven or braided bracelet.

## How is Raksha Bandhan celebrated?

This is how eleven-year-old Anita explains what happens during this ceremony.

A girl tying a rakhi on her brother's wrist

> I get up early in the morning and have my bath. My brother Anil, who is 13 years old, also does the same. My mother has a stainless steel tray ready. On it are some candies called *barfi*. There is also some *kum kum* (red powder) and some grains of rice. Finally, there is a rakhi which I chose especially for him.
>
> To begin with, I take the kum kum paste with my finger and put a round mark with it on his forehead. Next, I take some grains of rice and put them on the mark. After this, I take the rakhi and tie it around Anil's right wrist. As I am doing this, I say a little prayer: 'May God save you from illness and accidental death. May all your ambitions come true. May God bless you.'
>
> Then I take the barfi and put it in Anil's mouth. It's just as well that he likes sweets! I think he likes this part best of all. Anil now makes a promise to look after me, to protect me from harm. This year, he gave me a beautiful gold necklace as a present. Usually he gives me some money. I wouldn't mind if he didn't give me anything—as long as he continues to take care of me!
>
> – *Anita*

This is what Anil says about Raksha Bandhan.

> I really look forward to Raksha Bandhan. It is a way of showing our love for one another. We don't always get along with one another. Sometimes we argue about silly things, really, but we make up soon afterwards—with our parents' help! This year, my mom and I went shopping to buy Anita a gold necklace. I'm glad she likes it! I like my rakhi. I keep it tied around my wrist, until it falls off by itself. Sometimes this does not happen for a couple of weeks. People at school ask me about the rakhi. I tell them it is there to protect me from harm. I also explain that I have promised to look after my sister.
>
> *– Anil*

## The story of Indra and the demon king

Hindu children are reminded of the following story at the time of Raksha Bandhan.

A long time ago, a wicked demon king called Bali fought with a god named Indra. Bali drove Indra out of his kingdom. When this happened, Indra's wife, Sachi, was very upset. So she went to see the great God Vishnu to ask for help. Sachi was given a bracelet, made from some threads, to tie around Indra's wrist. When Indra fought another battle with the demon king, the bracelet gave him good luck and protection. Indra defeated the demon king and won back his kingdom.

*Indra protected by his rakhi*

# Raksha Bandhan Symbols

A selection
of rakhis

## What kind of rakhis are there?

There are many kinds of **rakhis**. Some are very simple, such as a red thread made out of cotton or silk. Others have more colorful decorations. Some have tinsel around them, and others have a plastic flower or beads joined onto the thread. Some Hindus like rakhis which have an **aum** or a **swastika** sign on them. To Hindus, a swastika is a sign for good health and fortune. It is drawn at the time of new beginnings. These signs remind Hindus of God and of the need for good health.

## Celebrating with cousins

Of course, not all Hindus have brothers or sisters. What do they do on Raksha Bandhan day? Hindu families are part of a larger group of families, made up of grandparents, uncles, aunts, and cousins. This kind of family is called an extended family. All members may not live together in one house. In Western countries like the United States, families may live close to each other. In the villages of India, larger extended Hindu families share one household.

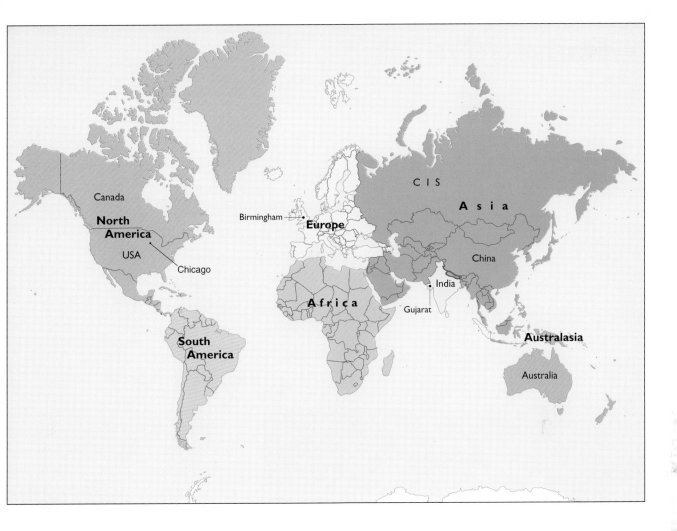

Wherever they live, Hindus feel that their cousins are also their brothers and sisters. On Raksha Bandhan day a girl will also tie rakhis around her male cousins' wrists.

Rohini lives in Chicago. She has no brothers. This is what she says about Raksha Bandhan.

> I don't have a brother. But I still get excited about tying a rakhi. My uncle lives in Gujarat, India. They have two sons who are the same age as me—ten years old. They are twins. I send them rakhis in the mail. We have to remember to do this long before the Raksha Bandhan day. I wish I could send them candy, too, but it would probably get squashed! Anyway, my aunt in India gives them candy and ties the rakhis for me. The twins usually send me a small gift. I think this is a good way to remember each other. One day I shall go to see them and tie a rakhi myself!
> – *Rohini*

# Mahashivaratri

Some Hindu children learn to dance at an early age. Hema lives in south India. One of her favorite gods is called Shiva. Shiva is sometimes worshiped as "the Lord of the Dance." This is what Hema says about Shiva.

*An image of Shiva as Lord of the Dance*

## What is Mahashivaratri?

Mahashivaratri is a solemn festival to honor Lord Shiva. *Shivaratri* means "the night of Shiva" and this is celebrated monthly when the new moon appears. *Mahashivaratri* means "the great night of Shiva" and takes place in January or February each year. It is on this night that Shiva is believed to perform a special dance.

One of the most famous images of Shiva is that of him dancing. Here he is known as *Shiva Nataraja*, or "Lord of the Dance." In this dance he destroys the old world so that a new world can be born. Hindus believe that when a person dies, he or she is born again into a new body. This is called *reincarnation*. Shiva's dance shows the cycle of birth, death, and being born again.

If you look closely at the picture of Shiva you can see that he has four hands. This is to show his power. In one hand he holds a small drum. In another hand he holds a flame. The drum represents the first sound of creation. The fire represents the end of the world. Hindus are not afraid of death. It is part of life. They believe that death means a new birth and another chance to grow closer to God.

A professional Hindu dancer

## Hindu dances

Dance is important in the Hindu religion. It is a way of enjoying the many stories linked with Hindu festivals. It also teaches people about some of the truths of their religion. The dances are colorful and full of fun. There is always a demon for the gods to defeat. The demon stands for evil in the world and its defeat shows that good will always win over evil in the end.

The dancers have to train for many years before they are able to perform their dances. There are some very difficult steps and gestures that have to be learned and practiced. Some of the hand gestures have special meanings and must be done in a particular way, otherwise they would give off a completely different meaning. Some Hindu dancers have become very famous throughout the world and many Hindus travel miles to see them.

# Images of Lord Shiva

*An image of Shiva prepared for the festival of Mahashivaratri. The Shiva Linga coming out of the lotus flower is made from butter.*

Apu, aged nine, lives in New York City. His family worships Shiva. This is what he says about it.

> **We have an image of Lord Shiva in our shrine at home. We also have a small poster showing Lord Shiva and his wife Parvati. They are with their son Ganesha and Nandi, the white bull.**
>
> – *Apu*

## Images of Shiva

Mahashivaratri is a festival when images of Shiva are given special respect. Some images show Shiva with his wife, Parvati. You can normally recognize Shiva by the *trident* (a three-pronged spear) he holds. He also has a special sign on his forehead of three horizontal lines. People who worship Shiva also paint this mark on their foreheads. Sometimes, Shiva and Parvati will be shown with two other figures. One is Ganesha, the elephant-headed god. He is Shiva and Parvati's son. You can read more about him on pages 40–41. The other is a white bull called Nandi, who is the animal Shiva rides.

During Mahashivaratri a special ceremony takes place. The picture shows milk being poured over a small stone column called a **Shiva Linga**. This is to honor Shiva. Here is a story to explain why the Shiva Linga is used.

*Milk being poured over a Shiva Linga. Can you see Nandi, the white bull, sitting facing Shiva?*

## The story of the Shiva Linga

One day, the gods Brahma and Vishnu were having an argument. They were quarreling about which one of them was the greatest. Suddenly a column of light appeared before them. It was huge, so they decided to have a race to see who could find the end of the column first. Brahma turned into a goose and flew up towards the sky to get to the top of the column. Vishnu turned himself into a boar and dove into the earth to get to the bottom of the column. Brahma flew up and up, but could not find the top. Vishnu dove deeper and deeper, but never got to the bottom. They were both exhausted. Suddenly they heard a loud voice: "I am the Lord Shiva. I am so great that you will never find my beginning or my end!" Vishnu and Brahma could not argue. All they could do was worship Shiva.

This is why many Hindus use a Shiva Linga when they worship Shiva. It reminds them of the column of light and the greatness of Shiva.

# Durgapuja

In each of her ten hands, Durga holds one of the gods' special weapons. For example, she holds Shiva's trident, a bow and arrow, a thunderbolt, and a conch shell.

Hindus also worship God in the form of a mother goddess. She has many names. One of her names is *Durga*. The festival of Durgapuja (**puja** means "worship") takes place during September and October. In India, it is a time when the rainy season is over. The rains help the crops grow and people look forward to harvesttime.

This is what Avni, aged nine, says about Durga.

" **Durga is married to the god Shiva. She has five pairs of arms. This is a way of saying that Durga is very powerful. By using her powers, she defeats evil forces. During the festival of Durgapuja, Hindus remember the story of how she fought with the buffalo demon called Mahisha. It is also a time when girls are given presents and are shown special respect.**
*– Avni* "

## The story of Durga and the buffalo demon

Brahma, the creator god, had agreed with Mahisha, the buffalo demon, that only a woman could kill him. This delighted the demon, because it was hard to imagine how a woman could kill a demon as strong as Mahisha. So he went around doing bad things. Soon the gods were fed up. They went to see the god Shiva and asked for his help. It was decided that Durga should fight the demon. She was armed with some special weapons which the gods themselves used.

Durga rode on a lion when she went to meet Mahisha. When he saw Durga, he laughed. He couldn't see how a woman could kill him. But when Durga destroyed many of the demon's warriors, he knew that he was in danger. So he turned into a fierce buffalo and charged at Durga. As the battle raged, Mahisha began to turn back into his demon form. When this happened, Durga struck him with a special spear and killed him. Everyone was glad that at last the evil demon had been destroyed. Peace and goodness came over the land, because of Durga. The victory of good over evil is what is celebrated at Durgapuja.

*Durga prepares to fight Mahisha*

# Navratri and Dassehra

*Hindus dancing around a shrine of the mother goddess*

## Navratri

In Gujarat, the western part of India, the festival of Durgapuja is known by a different name. It is called *Navratri*, which means "nine nights." The celebrations are different, too, although the mother goddess is still worshiped. Here she is called *mataji*, which means "honored mother." Dancing around the shrine of the goddess is the main way of celebrating. People of all ages dance for nine nights. It is a time of great fun. Hindus in the United States, for example, go to temples to dance and worship. Sometimes banquet halls are used. Children love to meet their friends and relatives. It is a treat to stay up till late at night! Foods such as fruit and candies are offered to the goddess for her blessings. At the end of each night's dancing this food, called **prashad,** is passed around and eaten by all.

An effigy of
Ravana ready
to be burned

## Dassehra

The celebration of the mother goddess is called *Dassehra* in northern India. Hindus believe this event is a good time to make a new start, such as buying a new house. People also give each other presents. Sanjay says this about Dassehra.

" **This is my favorite festival. People act out the story of Rama and Sita in the streets. The best part is when Ravana, the demon king, is defeated by Rama. A huge effigy of the ten-headed demon is made out of straw and cardboard. It is stuffed with fireworks. We help to build a bonfire around the effigy. Then it is set on fire. Everybody cheers as it burns! You should hear the fireworks going off. It's great!**"
– *Sanjay*

Dassehra is also celebrated in other parts of the world where Hindus have made their homes. In Nairobi, East Africa, an effigy of Ravana is built in a park. It is set on fire in the evening. Big crowds gather. It is very noisy and colorful. Hindu children, especially, have a wonderful time. It is also a reminder to them that goodness can conquer evil.

# Ramnavami

An image of Rama in a cradle in the mandir

For the festival of Ramnavami, Hindu families visit a **mandir**. Shantu, aged eight, likes going to the mandir. This is what she says about Ramnavami.

"  **At Ramnavami our family goes to the mandir. We put an image of baby Rama into a cradle. Then we sing songs until his birth at midday.** "
– *Shantu*

## What is Ramnavami?

Ramnavami is a festival to celebrate the birth of Rama. Rama is the hero of the famous story of **Ramayana**. Ramnavami takes place around March–April on the ninth day of the Hindu lunar month. It lasts for one day and is a day of fasting. On this occasion no salt, grains, or vegetables are eaten. The food allowed is made with sugar and yogurt.

*The ten
avatars of the
God Vishnu*

During this festival, passages from the Ramayana are read. You can read more about this story on pages 12–13. At this festival cradles are made and placed in the mandir. Then an image of the baby Rama is placed in the cradle and covered. The image stays covered until noon, which is when Rama is said to have been born. In some parts of India, images of both Rama and his wife Sita are carried through the village.

## Why is Rama special?

Rama was not just a famous prince. Like Krishna, he is believed to be the God Vishnu. Hindus believe that Vishnu appeared on earth in different forms to make sure that goodness and truth always would defeat the powers of evil and darkness. Each of Vishnu's appearances on earth is known as an **avatar**. This word means "to descend." Vishnu has descended to earth nine times and is due to come again in the future (the tenth avatar).

## The ten avatars

1. Vishnu appeared as Matsya the fish to warn humanity about a great flood.

2. In another story about a flood, Vishnu came to earth as Kurma the tortoise.

3. Vishnu rescued the world from the demon Hiranyaksha, when he came down to earth as Varaha, the boar.

4. Vishnu appeared as half-man, half-lion (Narasinha the man-lion) in order to defeat a demon called Hiranyakasipu.

5. In this story, Vishnu appeared as a dwarf (Vamana) in order to teach King Bali a lesson. Bali was becoming too powerful for his own good. He was in danger of stealing the power of the gods.

6. Parasurama or Rama with an axe. Some warriors were becoming too powerful. With the help of Shiva's axe, Parasurama was able to defeat them and restore order.

7. Rama, the prince and hero of the Ramayana (see pages 12–13).

8. Krishna, the great teacher of the **Bhagavad Gita**. You can read more about him on pages 16–17 and 34–35.

9. Prince Siddhartha Guatama, who became the Buddha. He was a great teacher and became the founder of the Buddhist religion.

10. Kalki, the savior who is yet to come. Hindus believe that Vishnu will appear in the form of Kalki when this world ends and a new world is born. Kalki will appear riding a white horse. In his hand there will be a flaming sword. He will use this to destroy the wicked and create a new world.

# Janmashtami

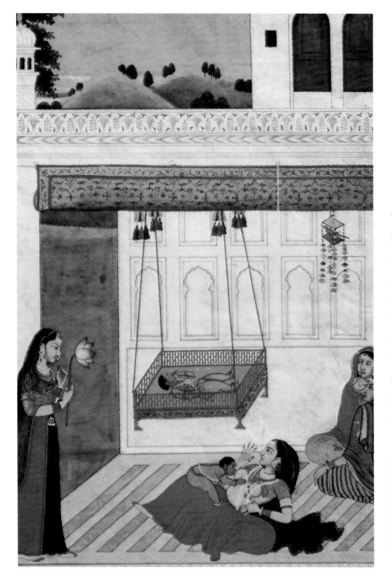

*Krishna as a baby in a cradle*

The festival of Lord Krishna's birth is called *Janmashtami*. It is celebrated in August or September. Krishna is one of the forms of the God Vishnu. Hindus believe that Krishna was born at midnight with the rising of the moon. People meet at the **mandir** and, as midnight draws near, there is a great sense of excitement in the air.

## Lord Krishna's teachings

Lord Krishna's teachings can be found in a special book called the **Bhagavad Gita**, which means "The Song of the Lord." In it, this is what Krishna says about people who make offerings to him: "Whoever offers me a leaf, a flower, a fruit or water with love, that offering of devotion I willingly accept from the pure of heart."

**What happens on Janmashtami?**
This is how ten-year-old Aruna describes the atmosphere.

*Baby Krishna*

" Our mandir is crowded and richly decorated. There are lots of children around. People are singing hymns called *bhajans* about Lord Krishna. I like the way the musicians, who play the harmonium (a keyboard instrument), cymbals, and tablas (small drums), try to keep up with the people singing! There is a cradle, decorated with silk cloth and flowers. In it is a model of the baby Krishna, looking very sweet.

Since this is a special day and night, our family does not eat any food. At midnight, everyone gathers to do *arti* with *diva* lamps at the cradle. All the children want to rock the cradle! Many gifts of fruit and candies have been brought by the worshipers. After midnight, this food, which is blessed by God, is passed around. I am feeling very hungry by this time—the food is welcome! A special drink called *charnamrit* is also given out. This is made out of milk, yogurt, sugar, water, and honey. It's delicious! I love to celebrate Janmashtami. It is dark outside, but in the mandir it is bright and full of life. It feels as if Lord Krishna is with us all. "
– *Aruna*

# Ratha Yatra

Bharti's family lives in the north of England. For some festivals they like to meet up with friends in London. One such festival is Ratha Yatra.

> " **Ratha Yatra is an important time for our family. We take a bus to London to join in the celebrations. There is a gigantic _rath_ (chariot), which we all take turns pulling. On the rath is a huge image of Lord Jagannath and his brother and sister. It's a really happy occasion.** "
>
> – _Bharti_

### What is Ratha Yatra?

Ratha Yatra is a popular festival in Puri, in northeast India. It takes place in June or July and hundreds of thousands of Hindus will join in the festival. It has also become an important festival in London, over the last few years. _Ratha Yatra_ means "the journey of the chariot." A huge rath, or chariot, is pulled through the town. It is a great honor to pull the rath and everybody will try to do it.

On the chariot there are three images. The main one is **Jagannath**, the Lord of the Universe. The others are his brother, Balarama, and his sister, Subhadra.

_The raths being pulled through the streets of Puri, have images of Jagannath, Balarama and Subhadra._

The word *juggernaut* is used in England to describe a huge truck. This word comes from the name Jagannath, who is seated on the great chariot. Jagannath is another name for Krishna, whom many Hindus think of as the Lord of the Universe. So on this day stories of Krishna are told and songs to Krishna are sung.

## How the image of Jagannath was made

Once there was a king who really wanted to see God. After many years of searching, he was told that Lord Jagannath would appear as a piece of wood. When he eventually found this wood, it was a huge tree trunk! Nobody could lift it until a holy man appeared out of nowhere and picked it up, as if it were a small branch. He took the wood to a hut where it could be carved into the image of God. But nobody could carve the tree. All their tools were blunted on the strong wood. The mysterious holy man reappeared and agreed to carve the wood, as long as he could do it in secret. The king agreed, but after waiting five days and five nights he became so curious that he burst into the hut. The holy man had gone. There was only an image of Lord Jagannath. It was unfinished. The holy man had vanished before he could carve Lord Jagannath's hands and feet.

### Wreaths

*Beautiful wreaths of flowers decorate the rath and the images of Jagannath, Balarama, and Subhadra. Wreaths are a sign of respect and you can often see them being used in Hindu worship. Flower wreaths are also given to important people, such as holy men and women and religious teachers.*

*A Hindu stonemason carving an image of a deity*

# Saraswati Puja

The first day of spring is marked by the festival of Vasant Panchami. It is celebrated in January or February. This day is especially dedicated to Saraswati, the goddess of learning and wisdom. Saraswati is also important to Hindus because she is linked with the arts, especially poetry and music. On this day, Saraswati is worshiped by people who play music for those who have gathered to celebrate.

## How is Saraswati worshiped?

Bright yellow clothes are worn. Yellow is a royal color and also stands for the warmth of spring. In Bengal eastern India, large images of Saraswati are taken out in big parades. Musicians play loud, happy music through the streets. After the images of Saraswati have been worshiped, they are placed in the river. The name *Saraswati* means "the flowing one," and this goddess was thought to live in the holy Saraswati River.

*Pictures of Saraswati show her as a beautiful goddess. She is shown playing a stringed instrument called a* veena. *Sometimes she is shown sitting on a lotus flower or riding on a dazzlingly white swan. Both are symbols of purity.*

## Musical celebrations

Sometimes music and folk dances are an important part of festival celebrations and worship. Viren describes some of the instruments that are used.

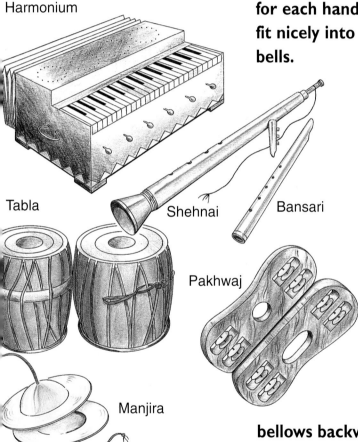

Harmonium

Tabla

Shehnai

Bansari

Pakhwaj

Manjira

A harmonium (a reed organ), a shehnai (a wind instrument), a bansari, tabla, pakhwaj (two pieces of wood with bells or brass plates attached, used like castanets), and manjira

" A *veena* is a stringed instrument. It looks a bit like a sitar. It is quite big. People sit down to play it by holding it upright. It makes a sweet, heavenly sound, reminding me of the sound of a harp.

A *khundjri* is like a tambourine. You hold it in one hand and use the other hand to hit the skin of the instrument rhythmically.

*Manjira* are brass castanets. You have one for each hand. They are quite small and they fit nicely into your hands. They sound like bells.

*Tabla* are drums, usually played as a pair. You have to sit down to play them. There are other drums which can be carried around in one hand. These are used in parades—for example, during Divali celebrations.

A *harmonium* is a keyboard instrument. It is played while sitting down. It does not need to be tuned and is not too hard to play. The musician plays the notes on the keyboard with one hand and moves the bellows backward and forward with the other hand.

My favorite instrument is a flute called a *bansari*. Pictures of Lord Krishna often show him playing a bansari. The sound is pure and it makes the hair on the back of my neck stand on end! "
– *Viren*

# Ganesha Chaturti

Many Hindu families have a favorite "family" god or gods. Images of the god Ganesha can be found in almost all Hindu homes. For Sanjay, aged ten, Ganesha is very special.

> **Ganesha is one of our favorite deities. We always pray to Ganesha before a special event like a wedding or a test.**
> – *Sanjay*

*Indian elephants clearing a forest of fallen trees*

### Who is Ganesha?

You will often see an image of Ganesha in a Hindu house. The letter *a* is not pronounced in Ganesha. He is a very popular **deity** and is easily recognized by his elephant head. Ganesha Chaturti is a festival which is very popular in western India. This festival celebrates the birth of Ganesha. It takes place during August or September.

Ganesha is the son of Shiva and Parvati. He is the "remover of obstacles." In India elephants are used to clear tree trunks and other obstacles from the forest roads. When people pray to Ganesha, they ask him to remove obstacles which would stop life from running smoothly. Before getting married, or before any major event like a driver's test or a school exam, Hindus will pray to Ganesha.

Here is a picture of Ganesha. In his hands Ganesha holds a lotus blossom, an axe, and a plate of laddoos (his favorite candy). His fourth hand is raised to give a blessing.

## How Ganesha got his head

There are many stories about how Ganesha received his elephant head. Here is one of them.

When Ganesha was born Parvati was so proud of him that she invited all the gods to come and admire him. Unfortunately, one of the guests was Sari, who was wicked. Sari was so jealous of this beautiful baby that she burnt Ganesha's head to ashes with the power of her gaze.

You can imagine Parvati's grief when she saw what had happened to her new baby. She pleaded with Brahma, the creator, to give her baby a new head. He agreed to replace the baby's head with the head of the first living creature he could find. It was an elephant.

### Prayer to Ganesha

The name of Ganesha is repeated at the start of many things, such as a journey, a marriage, or even a letter.
Here is an example of a prayer to Ganesha.
"**Aum** Lord Ganesha, dressed in white, with four arms.
Your color is that of the moon and your face is full of joy.
We worship you so that all obstacles may be removed."

# Other Festivals

This book has looked at the main Hindu festivals. But there are many other festivals enjoyed by Hindus all over the world.

*Hindus bathing in the Ganges River*

## Ugadi

Ugadi is a New Year festival. In some parts of India, it is a public holiday. On this day people rub their bodies with perfumed oil. After bathing, they wear new clothes. It is believed that Brahma created the world on this day. So it is a day for new beginnings, such as building a house or starting a job. As a sign of welcome, people make a string of mango leaves and hang it across the top of their front doors.

## Pongal

Pongal is a three-day festival. It is celebrated in southern India. It is a time when people give thanks to God for their crops and for the rain and sun which help the crops to grow. Rice and milk, mixed with sugar, is boiled and offered to the sun god Surya. *Pongal* means "it is boiled."

Cows are also respected. They are especially important to farmers. Cows are washed and wreaths of leaves and flowers are hung around their necks. They are allowed to graze anywhere they like!

| Decorated cows in India

## Celebrating festivals

Children all over the world enjoy festivals. Hindu children are no different! They love having fun, dressing up, and giving and receiving presents. This is what Geeta, aged 9, says about celebrating Hindu festivals.

Ashok is 10 years old. This is what he says about why festivals are important to him.

❝ **We have so many festivals it is hard to remember them all! Since we live in India, some of the festivals are holidays. We visit friends, decorate our houses and eat special food. Best of all, I like to learn and remember the stories about gods and goddesses. During some festivals, these stories are acted out in public. It is very exciting! Celebrating festivals reminds us that God is everywhere.** ❞
*– Geeta*

❝ **It is not easy to be a Hindu if you don't live in India. But especially at festival times in the United States, our family and friends celebrate well. We have great fun and good food. As I grow older, I understand more about why we celebrate. I have learned that our religion teaches us to be kind to everybody and to be thankful to God for everything.** ❞
*– Ashok*

# Glossary

**arti** performed during worship, when cotton wicks (divas) are lit in front of images of gods and goddesses and moved in a circle, accompanied by the singing of a special hymn.

**aum** (sometimes written *om*). The most sacred sound and sign for Hindus; the sound of God. Hindus believe that the universe began with this sound, and it is usually the first sacred word that a newborn baby hears.

**avatar** "descent to earth." How God comes to earth to destroy evil and to restore goodness in the world. The God Vishnu has had nine avatars, including the forms of Rama and Krishna, who are among the most popular Hindu gods.

**Bhagavad Gita** one of the most popular Hindu scriptures, meaning "The Song of the Lord." Contains the teachings of Lord Krishna. Many Hindus read parts of the Bhagavad Gita every day.

**bhajan** special songs and hymns which are recited by worshipers at home and as a part of worship in a mandir. The singing is often accompanied by music played on instruments such as harmoniums, and tablas (drums).

**brahmin** a member of the priestly group of Hindus. Not all brahmins are priests. Hindus believe that brahmins have special duties and responsibilities towards God and all creation.

**charnamrit** a special drink which is drunk by worshipers during the celebrations of Krishna's birth. It is made from milk, sugar, water, yogurt, and honey. Using a teaspoon, worshipers put a little bit of this drink in the palm of their hand, and drink it, asking for Krishna's blessing.

**deity** another word used for God, gods or goddesses.

**diva** a twisted raw-cotton wick, which is dipped in melted purified butter (ghee) and placed in a lamp. During worship, a diva is lit and placed in front of the gods and goddesses being worshiped. Many divas are lit during the festival of Divali.

**ghee** butter melted down and made pure. Ghee is used during religious ceremonies when a small fire is lit and fed with ghee. Ghee is also used during daily worship, when divas are lit.

**gopis** milkmaids or cowgirls who are mentioned in stories about Krishna. These wives and daughters of cowherders played and danced with Krishna and showed their love for him by becoming devoted to him.

**Jagannath** another name for the deity Krishna, whom many Hindus think of as the Lord of the Universe.

**kum kum** a red or orange-yellow powder which is made into a paste by using a little water. This paste is used to make a mark on a worshiper's forehead. It is also used to make a mark on a deity during worship.

**mandir** a place of worship for Hindus, sometimes called a temple. In the United States, a mandir can also be used by Hindu communities as a place for meetings and for having weddings.

**mendhi** sometimes called henna; a paste made from crushed leaves. Nowadays it can be bought as a dark brown powder. Mendhi is used to make decorative patterns on the hands, and sometimes the feet, of girls and adult women. This is done during the festival of Divali and at the time of engagements and weddings.

**prashad** food which is blessed by God and then eaten by worshipers.

**puja** an act of worship or devotion. This can take place in a mandir and at home. Many Hindu homes have a special area, called a shrine. Here there are images, called *murtis*, of gods and goddesses, as well as other items used during worship.

**rakhi** a bracelet, usually made out of cotton threads and sometimes decorated with tinsel. A rakhi is tied by a sister to her brother's wrist during the festival of Raksha Bandhan.

**Ramayana** one of the important Hindu scriptures, or holy books, which tells the story of Rama and his wife Sita. The story of Divali comes from the Ramayana.

**rangoli** sometimes called *alpana*; a pattern made to decorate the entrances of homes and mandirs, using colored chalk. Sometimes rice is also used. Rangoli patterns are made especially during the festivals of Divali and Holi, as a way of welcoming deities and visitors.

**rath** a large vehicle, sometimes a chariot, which is used to carry large images of gods and goddesses. It is used during the festival of Ratha Yatra, when a chariot is pulled through the streets.

**sanatan dharma** "eternal religion"; the words used by Hindus to describe their faith.

**Sanskrit** an ancient Indian language, sacred to Hindus.

**Shiva Linga** "Shiva sign" (*linga* means "sign"); a pillar, rounded at the top, which can be made of wood, metal or stone. It is usually found in mandirs in which Shiva is worshiped.

**swastika** an ancient Indian sign of peace, well-being and good fortune. Often it is found painted as a design on a mandir wall. The four lines of a swastika stand for the directions of the compass. This is also a way of saying that God can be reached using different paths.

# More Books to Read

*Hinduism.* Dilip Kadodwala; Thomson Learning, 1995.

*Hinduism.* Madu B. Wangu; Facts on File, 1991.

*Way of the Hindu.* Swami Yogeshanananda; Dufour, 1980.

*Let's Celebrate Autumn.* Mike Rosen, ed. Deb Elliott; Wayland (Publishers) Ltd., 1994.

*Let's Celebrate Spring.* Mike Rosen, ed. Deb Elliott; Wayland (Publishers) Ltd, 1994.

*Let's Celebrate Summer.* Mike Rosen, ed. Deb Elliott; Wayland (Publishers) Ltd., 1994.

*Let's Celebrate Winter.* Mike Rosen, ed. Deb Elliott; Wayland (Publishers) Ltd., 1994.

*Understanding Religions: Food and Fasting.* Deidre Burke, Wayland (Publishers) Ltd., 1992.

*Understanding Religions: Pilgrimages and Journeys.* Katherine Prior, Wayland (Publishers) Ltd., 1992.

# A Closer Look

This picture shows children dancing a scene from the
Ramayana, a book popular with Hindus everywhere. An
important story in this book is that of Prince Rama and
his wife Sita. Rama defeats the ten-headed demon
Ravana to rescue his wife and regain his country (see
pages 12–13). The new King and Queen are welcomed
back and diva lamps light up their path. The story shows
Hindus how good will always conquer evil and is
celebrated at the Divali festival through dance or drama.

# Index